How To Dress Like It's The Sixties

By Mandy Morello

Contents

A Note From The Author

When I was young enough to wear jelly shoes, I saw a video of Courtney Love flouncing around her Seattle home with a cigarette, pulling dresses out from her closet and gushing about how much she loves them.

She pulled out lots of dresses that she customised herself and proudly showed the camera her battered designer shoes. She talked excessively about what she had done to each dress, where she found them and proudly stated, "It's vintage. Most of my clothes are vintage."

I was amazed. I was only young at the time but I wanted to know more about this 'vintage' stuff. So I jumped on my family computer, waited for that surgical dial-up noise to be over and asked my virtual online butler, Jeeves, where the closest vintage shop was. And that's the day I fired my first (and only) butler.

He obnoxiously told me, I would have to travel to bigger cities to find real vintage. But I couldn't afford that, I was just a child. I didn't have a job. So I gave up and gave in to a life of Claire's Accessories and Tammy Girl instead.

A couple of years later, I moved to London and thought I had hit the vintage jackpot. Not only did I find regular vintage markets but there was a vintage shop conveniently located right next to my new university.

The shop was called Blue 17 and they had arranged lots of their clothes by the decade. It was there, in that shop, that I fell in love with sixties clothes. The first item I bought in that shop was a houndstooth sixties mod skirt. It was the perfect fit and shape.

Before I knew it, I had suitcases filled with sixties clothes and I treated each one of them as if they're my babies. They all have their unique quirks, backgrounds and stories that I could talk endlessly about over a glass of wine. Eventually, I found that sixties clothes aren't only found in a big city, but everywhere.

All I needed when I was younger was a guide better than Jeeves. And that's why I'm writing this book. I'm gonna help you dress like it's the sixties authentically.

1. An Affair With Sixties Fashion

I went into my first vintage shop one gloomy day in London. I had walked past it a few times, eyeing up the brunette fur coats in the window. But on that rainy day, it was cold outside and I had a few moments to kill, so I made the excuse, plucked up the courage and walked inside.

The woman behind the counter looked up and smiled briefly while she continued her phone conversation. The shopfront had cosy, dim lighting and the place smelled like wood. I walked slowly to the first rack of clothes and began thumbing through, pretending I knew what I was looking at.

I picked up a gorgeous blazer with pale pink flower prints on it. I'd never seen anything like it. It was beige with black thin stripes. The flowers had been printed in random order and the material felt strong. Attached to the arm was a tag that read '60s Blazer'.

I was shocked for two reasons. I thought the only patterns they had in the sixties were psychedelic or monochrome geometric styles. And how can something as old as Philip Schofield look so unweathered?

Turns out, I shouldn't have been shocked at all. Sixties fashion was much more than what we see in the costume store. It can be modern, classy and timeless. But it can also be avant-garde, daring and unique. For something I thought could be so easily defined by a couple of looks, was so much more.

The sixties was the beginning of modern fashion as we know it now. It was the first time women were wearing what they wanted and when they wanted. If they wanted to wear anything at all, that is. But everyone's thoughts about how a woman should dress hadn't changed overnight. The majority of men (and a few women) thought we should dress and behave as they had done in the 1950s. Which makes every young woman, who dared to wear short skirts, a hero in my book.

Marianne Faithful

Turn On

Fashion wasn't the only thing that progressed in the sixties. If you turned on the radio in the 1960s, the music would have blown your mind. You would have heard The Beatles, Rolling Stones, Led Zeppelin, Jimi Hendrix, Janis Joplin, Dusty Springfield, Tina Turner and so many more. Musicians were the new idols.

To pledge their loyalty to their favourite bands, they dressed like them. They'd pick up the latest magazines and copy their looks, or even their girlfriend's looks. Then they'd go to the bars (or the brand new discos) that played their favourite music and danced all night, showing off their handmade versions of Francoise Hardy's dress.

It must come as no surprise to you that the very first band t-shirts had begun to be printed in the sixties. Everyone was keen to show who they listened to because music became the new religion.

Tune In

A new drug began to circulate - LSD. When everyone's favourite musicians had admitted to trying it, the drug went mainstream for most of the era. The side effects of the drug were strong hallucinations and distorted sound. Many people tried to replicate their LSD experiences in their art, music and fashion.

This in turn began to push the boundaries of clothes. Designers tried new patterns, colours and fabrics to represent the mood of the moment. Paisley, tye die and bold florals became popular. And not just the designers were feeling inspired. Women were wearing clothes borrowed from other cultures such as Morocco, India and Eastern Asia. Fashion was truly broadening its horizons.

Drop Out

Women in the fifties were expected to look pretty, know how to clean and be absolutely charming at all times. Their goal was to find a man and have children with him. And if you didn't achieve that goal, you were labelled a hag.

After decades of these forced expectations and suppressed dreams, some women decided to drop out. Some decided to run away to communes while others ran away to write poetry about their suppressions. They gave up their corsets and make-up in exchange for a life free from the pressures of modern-day society and capitalism. They refused to join in the money game and instead, found their wealth from within.

But other women dropped out in another way. They refused to give up on their dreams and instead joined the men in the workplace. They began entering all-boy universities, applying for 'male roles' and becoming the boss. They needed smart clothes and suits to make themselves look and feel the part. They faced an incredible amount of sexism, way more than we experience today, but they persevered. And for the first time, women began to have their own money.

After researching sixties fashion, I realised that one floral blazer took me down a rabbit hole from which I would never return. Are you ready?

2.
Traditional Style Rules

For years I tried to pack my body into high waisted jeans. They're fashionable, they're vintage-style and they make other girl's butts look amazing. But, they never made my butt look amazing and I couldn't work out why. Maybe I wasn't buying good quality jeans? Maybe I wasn't buying the right colour? Maybe I was wearing the wrong top with them? Maybe I'm just not skinny enough...?

It was none of the above. According to traditional body shapes, high waisted jeans did not look good on me because I have what you would call a 'boyish' shape or 'rectangle'. My waist isn't very defined which means high waisted jeans make me look like a DVD case.

Rather than get upset by this knowledge, I felt liberated. Knowing my body shape and learning what suits it stops me from buying clothes that don't. I bet you have a few things in your wardrobe that you've bought and never worn because it doesn't look quite right on you.

In the sixties, it was the first time that designers were making the clothes to fit the woman's body rather than making the woman fit the clothes. They began to focus on five traditional female body types and designed clothes that would flatter them. And it was all achieved with the fashion principle of balance.

Step one: Measure yourself.

Measure your bust, waist and hips. These are the most important measurements you'll need when it comes to finding the perfect clothes for you. It's also handy to measure your arm length, leg length, body length and shoulders. Write it all down on your phone somewhere you can easily access it wherever you are. Remember, weight loss or weight gain can distort these figures so it's important to keep these updated.

Step Two: Find your body shape.

Once you've got your measurements, have a look at these five traditional body shape categories and work out which one sounds most like you.

- Are your bust & hips a similar size? If they're within 5% of each other and your waist is less than 25% smaller, welcome to the boyish club, my girl. The key characteristic of a boyish shape is that the body is straight up and down with no definition. A 'boyish' girl's best asset is usually those great pins.

- If you're bottom-heavy you're a pear. The main feature of a pear is a gorgeous big bottom. Your hips will be over 5% bigger than your bust and your waist will be the smallest measurement. You'll want to flaunt your tiny waist while making your top half appear bigger.

- Heart shapes are the opposite of a pear. Is your bust 5% bigger than your hip measurement? What about your shoulder measurement? The key feature of a heart is a bigger upper body. You'll want to make your butt appear bigger to balance your fabulous assets.

- To be an hourglass, your waist has to be 25% smaller than your bust and hips. And your bust and your hips are practically the same sizes. You can easily spot an hourglass by the wider hips and bust with a pinched-in waist like a wasp.

- If your waist is the same or wider than your bust, you're an apple, my friend. Usually, the hips will be the smallest of all the measurements with the key feature being a wider waist. You'll want to define the waist and conceal those small hips.

If you don't feel like you fit into these body shape categories, that's ok, they are more traditional shapes and don't reflect all modern-day women. Focus on the parts of your body that you want to show off, and this will help with the next step.

Step Three: What To Wear.

Now you have a body shape in mind or a part of your body that you want to focus on, you can start figuring out what will look great on. It's all about balance, remember.

Dressing A Boyish Figure

Clothes that will create curves and make that undefined waist look slimmer:

- Tops with bateau necklines

- Turtlenecks and long thick jumpers

- Off the shoulder dresses

- Flared sleeves and pussy-bow blouses.

- Longer coats like pea coats, dusters or trenches that are tied up by the waist.

- Stay away from anything high waisted and embrace low waisted or mid-rise hareem pants and slim trousers.

- Full, pencil and skirts. Use them in bright colours and print.

- Shift, princess seams and empire dresses. Extra marks if there's a dark colour around the waist.

- Belted playsuits

- Secret weapon: Knee high socks paired with a-line miniskirts

Dressing a Pear Figure

Clothes that add more weight to the top half of your body:

- Wear a good push up bra
- Tops with cowl, Sabrina and square necklines.
- Turtleneck jumpers
- Big short sleeves
- Crop tops and cropped jackets
- Short fur coats & shawls
- Shirts tied at the waist
- Dark empire line and princess coats
- Dark high waisted jeans
- High rise flares with no pockets on the booty.
- Knee-length high waisted skirts that are bias cut or panelled. Nothing too voluminous.
- Tulip and a-line dresses with collars
- Secret weapon: Big hair

Dressing A Heart Figure

Clothes that add more curves to the hips and butt, while celebrating the top half of the body:

- Tops with halternecks and deep, narrow necklines such as a V or scoop

- Wide straps

- Long fitted dark tops

- Wrap cardigans and belted blazers

- Trapeze Coats

- Light coloured flares, Palazzos and Harem pants

- Light coloured baggy & boyfriend jeans

- Box pleated and a-line skirts

- A-line, shift and cinched in waist dresses that flare out at the bottom

- Secret weapon: Platform shoes

Dressing An Hourglass Figure

Clothes that show off the body's natural silhouette:

- Tops with sweetheart, off the shoulder and square necklines
- Sleeveless or fitted sleeves on tops and blouses.
- Lightweight form-fitting knits and jumper dresses
- Fitted leather jacket or blazer
- Form fitted, simple coats that draw in at the waist
- High waisted slim or flare jeans
- High waisted pencil skirts or full circle skirts
- Dresses with a panelled waist, shift dresses and bias-cut dresses
- High waisted hot pants and capri pants
- Simple tailored catsuit
- Secret weapon: A waist belt

Dressing An Apple Figure

Clothes that define the waist and deemphasize the tummy:

- Strapless tops
- Low and wide necklines like deep Vs and sweetheart
- Tunics and swing tops with texture and interesting prints
- Poncho
- Simple, hip-length structured coats, without a belt
- Flare, flowy and wide low waisted trousers.
- Dark coloured, low waisted or mid-waisted flares.
- A-line or flared skirts that come above the knee.
- Baby doll dresses and smocks
- Bias cut, a-Line and shift dresses
- Secret weapon: Coloured tights

Go wild. Experiment. These body shape suggestions can work as a loose guide to help you find what suits your body through the fashion principle of balance. The best way to discover what looks good on you is through trial and error. Try things on, note down what looks great on you and what doesn't. I keep a mental list of things that look horrendous on me; high waisted jeans, square necklines and crop tops. The things that do suit me, I stock up on. That way, anytime you pull something out of your wardrobe, you know it will make you look and feel fabulous.

3. The Fashion Revolution

Three young girls from Brighton gathered for a sleepover on the 31st of December 1959. It was about to be the beginning of a new decade and the end of the 1950s. The girls discussed what they were going to do in the next ten years, hoping that it would be the best decade ever.

But things didn't look very good for the 14-year-old girls. They were destined, as all young girls were in England, to follow in the same path as their parents. After school, they would be expected to find a job, work until they found a man and raise his children.

"I don't wanna have children." one of them whined while pulling a sick face. "I wanna go to Egypt and become an Egyptologist. Being a mum looks terribly boring."

"I wanna be a jazz singer." one of the other girls cooed. "I'd sing Jazz so good that Sinatra will duet with me."

"Well I do want to have children," said the third girl, "But I want to have them in a nice big house with a closet full of pretty clothes. And... I'd have a TV!"

They continued discussing their dreams as they pulled on their coats and wandered out to the back garden. They were tired of being told they were too poor, too working-class and too female to do the things they wanted to do. Their dreams were only reserved for the very wealthy or men.

The clock suddenly struck midnight and their attention moved to the sky glittering with crackles and fireworks. It was officially the sixties. They held their breath and each made a wish, hoping that this would be the decade that everything would change. And it would.

1960

In the Spring, a lot of school girls wore their best dresses and fresh pantyhose to the cinema with their girlfriends. A lot of them were wearing the most popular style of dress; a fit and flare. Underneath they were wearing a corset to give the impression that their waist is tinier than it was. And if the ones from a respectable part of town, were wearing their matching gloves paired with a fabulous shade of lipstick to complete the look.

The girls were heading to the cinema to catch a new French film by Jean Luc Goddard. All the girls in school were gossiping about it. It was supposed to be cool, stylish and very, very French.

But there were some other girls in the queue for the cinema too and they were dressed very differently. These girls dressed in capri trousers with plain shirts and jumpers. Some wore dark eyeliner but wouldn't dream of wearing lipstick. They were called the Beatniks and they were the coolest cats around. Or so they thought.

"They dropped out of school." One of the girls in the queue whispered. "They'll be sorry when they can't afford to feed their children!"

But the beatniks didn't care about trivial things like that. They stood in the queue, smoking and discussing a poem they had heard last night in a cafe. Just like the beats in America, they rejected modern ideals like getting married and settling down. All those things were for 'squares'.

Unfortunately for the subculture, the things that the beatniks rejected, were starting to commercialise them. They were popping up in films, TV and even Dior's latest collection. Beatniks were becoming trendy.

That evening in Spring, the beatniks and the school girls piled into the cinema and found their seats. A hush went across them all as the film *A Bout De Souffle* began and no one uttered a word until it ended. It was a raw, intense movie that they had never seen before. And they all fell in love with the actress Jean Seberg. Her hair was short like a pixie. And her clothes were so timeless yet modern. She wore plain tops with trousers that appealed to the beatniks and a nautical striped dress that made the school girls swoon. And she was undeniably pretty. But it wasn't just her fashion that influenced. In the film, she discusses sleeping with other men so casually that it made sex seem cool.

1961

In November, a Welsh girl won the crown of Miss World. All eyes were on her as comedian Bob Hope placed the crown on her pretty little head. She was the first British beauty queen to win the title and her country was so proud. Little girls across the nation saw the news and began practising their beauty queen waves.

In the sixties, the glamour and poise of the fifties hadn't completely been washed away. A lot of women still wanted to look and dress like the ideal fifties housewife. They bought corsets to pull in their waist to look like Sophia Loren and Marilyn Monroe. They wore restrictive bras and powdered on their rosy cheeks. They groomed their hair into big bouffants and cemented it in place with a heavy amount of hair spray. They wanted to look their best to catch a man, or even keep the one they already had.

They often looked for magazine photos of Elizabeth Taylor or Jackie Kennedy for style inspiration. Although looking as polished as their idols was a lot of time and effort every single day, they believed it was worth it. A trip to the corner shop couldn't be done without a face full of makeup and a good dress.

Even though modern films were getting more experimental and pushing boundaries with their storylines, many of the popular ones were still projecting that Hollywood glamour. *Breakfast At Tiffany's* told the story of a very stylish independent woman but gives up her lifestyle for love. *La Dolce Vita* gave us a new Marilyn Monroe, Anita Ekberg. And the real Marilyn Monroe starred in her last film *The Misfits*.

But unlike the fifties, girls from any background felt like they had more of a chance of being a face after they watched Miss World. Especially a young country girl called Jean Shrimpton who was just offered the opportunity to model for Vogue magazine, a magazine that had only used upper-class models in the past.

1962

A controversial book was spotted in the hands of what seemed like a civilised young woman on the London tube. An old woman scoffed and a man cheered but the young girl didn't notice. She was too absorbed in the words of Helen Gurley Brown.

Her book *Sex And The Single Girl* was being read all over the world by young women. It gave various tips and tricks to being a young single girl. She covered controversial topics such as travelling to Europe alone, having a career and nonmarital sex. Helen celebrated being single, even if you were older than 25.

The young girl on the tube turned a page and smiled as she read the sentence 'You may marry or you may not. In today's world, that is no longer the big question for women.'

She felt such validation and sighed with relief as she put the book safely in her purse. The girl was dressed in a smart pencil skirt and matching lilac blazer. She checked her watch on which had previously belonged to a cockney guy that she met up with on Tuesday evenings.

The tube came to a halt and she stepped off in her kitten-heeled shoes. She was on her way to a job interview. She had dreams of making her own money, moving away from home and having a little flat of her own in the city. She had no desire to share it all with a man, it would be all her own.

1963

Eddie saw them come to his late-night coffee bar every evening. They'd ride in on their scooters, stay all night talking excitedly and listening to the loudest music they could find on the jukebox. He let them come in because it kept his business afloat, but he often wondered how they came to be his best clientele.

They were called 'Mods'. He'd read the term in a newspaper one day. It said they were a group of troublemakers and hooligans. Although it made Eddie nervous, *his* mods had never caused trouble in the coffee bar. They just came to discuss fashion, Top Of The Pops and French movies. In fact, he thought some of the women looked like Jean Seberg.

One Saturday night, while Eddie was polishing an espresso cup, a mod girl walked in and put some money in the jukebox before sitting at the bar. It was quite unusual because the mods only came in on the weekdays.

"Not with your friends this weekend?" Eddie said as he gave her a bottle of beer.

"Not this weekend Eddie. I had to stay to do some shopping on Carnaby street," she replied while taking a sip of her drink. She wore her hair in a bob with a blunt fringe. Her eyes were heavily painted and her hair was backcombed.

"Can I ask... where do you lot go on the weekends?" Eddie inquired.

"Oh, we all go to the seaside to hang out. Brighton's the usual."

Eddie smiled. They didn't sound like trouble makers at all. Just young teenagers having fun. Going to the seaside was one of Eddie's favourite things to do when he was a teenager too.

"I don't know why the papers write so badly 'bout your lot." He chuckled.

"Me neither Eddie." She placed her empty bottle down. "It's the rockers they should write about."

"The rockers?"

"Yeah," her face scrunched up like she'd just seen a turd. "They don't dress like us. They ride motorbikes and wear leather. Disgusting."

"Like greasers?" Eddie's smile faded. He remembered being beaten up by a greaser after a dance when he was young. The greaser was wearing head to toe leather and slick, combed hair. He grimaced at the memory of a biker boot hitting him in the stomach.

"Yeah, they're called rockers now. But same shit, different toilet. They come to Brighton just to fight with us. I don't want to mess up my dress but the boys get involved."

Eddie was quite angered by this. Angry at the greaser that beat him up and angry for the modern greasers that were beating up his mods.

'Well you mark my words." he said, throwing down his tea towel. "Your lot is always safe here. And if I see a rocker come into this cafe, he'll regret the day he was born."

The mod girl smiled as the music stopped and swiftly changed to the next track - The Beatles.

1964

Mrs Rosenberry thought she had seen almost everything. She was sixty years old, married and had two rosy-faced grandchildren. She'd lived through the depression, saw the rise of jazz, and lived through the war. She always liked to tell the story of how a bomb had dropped right near her home one time during the blitz. She'd seen heartache and she'd seen tragedy. She thought nothing could shock her anymore.

But one morning, when she went out to buy a newspaper and a bag of coconut mushrooms from the corner shop, she nearly fainted. She had walked past a girl with a lot of leg showing. Her skirt came several inches above the knee.

"She was practically naked!" she told her neighbour. "Honestly, the girl should have been ashamed of herself."

"Well these days, girls are dressing like little harlots, Mrs Rosenberry." Her neighbour replied casually while pulling out a cigarette. "Don't even think about going near the beaches these days. You'll have a heart attack."

"Surely they're not naked just like the baby Jesus?"

"No, that's still illegal." Her neighbour replied, taking a long drag. "But let's say the new beachwear don't leave a lot to the imagination."

Mrs Rosenberry gasped.

"I had to 'accidentally' spill ice cream on my husband's glasses so he wouldn't see. He was so angry with me but, you see, I didn't want him going astray, Mrs Rosenberry." She said with sadness in her eyes.

Mrs Rosenberry nodded, wondering what the world was coming to. Hemlines on skirts were getting shorter and bikinis were the new favourite thing to wear on the beach.

In the fashion world 'toplessness' was the new trend. Topless bikinis and topless dresses were showcased on runways and fashion magazines. But anyone who attempted wearing the designs in the real world would be met with a fine and a lot of appalled old ladies.

Designers were innovating at a rapid pace. Well-known designer Paco Rabanne brought out a collection of 'Twelve Experimental Dresses' and worked with a black model Donyale Luna. Because of his partnership with her and other black models, journalists spat in the well-respected designer's face. But, where fashion went, the rest of the world would eventually follow.

1965

Country girl Jean Shrimpton had done it. She had become the world's first supermodel featured on many front covers of Vogue and known even outside the fashion world. Newspapers reported that she was the highest-paid model too.

Dupont textiles dished out £2000 (huge money at the time) for Jean to fly to Australia and attend a Derby Day in Melbourne. That's more than the Beatles were paid for their Australian tour. Dupont sent her a roll of their fabric so that she could make a dress and advertise their business. Jean and her dressmaker decided on a simple shift dress and kept it a surprise until the day of the Derby.

Jean, excited to be in the hot Australian sun, stepped out on Derby Day waving at the crowd. She came out to deathly silence followed by a mixture of wolf whistles and howling. Confused, she carried on with presenting an award and quietly left.

The Australian press hounded her for her shift dress. They complained it was too short and were repulsed that she didn't wear gloves and pantyhose. Jean replied that Australia wasn't ready for her.

Miraculously the British press came to her aid and defended her short dress. To them, it was modern and elegant. They were outraged at the Australian treatment of their supermodel, showing that Britain's attitudes to fashion had indeed changed rapidly since the fifties. Shorter skirts were now acceptable.

1966

It was the first time Jenny was getting on a plane. She was the daughter of aristocrats and lived in a huge estate in the country. While her parents were happily exploring their acres, Jenny itched to see the world. She'd managed to persuade them to give her an allowance, which she spent immediately on plane tickets to Capris.

There was going to be a party in Capris, then a weekend in Ibiza and then cocktails in St Tropez. She couldn't wait to find out where the next party would take her.

For her first flight, she wore an Emilio Pucci matching trouser and top set. Her friend, who invited her to the party in Capris, had said that it's what all the cool people were wearing. The matching set had a swirling blueish print that looked like a kaleidoscope and was made with a material that felt so light. Perfect for plane travel.

When Jenny got on the plane, she was greeted by a heavily stylish woman, the air hostess. Being an air hostess had become such a glamorous job that even designers like Pucci had been designing their uniforms. If she didn't have any money, she would have been an air hostess, she thought.

Jenny was shown to her seat which was right by the window. As soon as she got comfortable, she pulled out one of her favourite magazines. Inside she spotted a picture of her friend dancing on a table in Rome on page 14. She couldn't wait to do that. There were also plenty of photos of Truman Capotes' black and white ball in New York. She hoped someday, she'd be invited to something like that. And then she noodled over a picture of Brigitte Bardot leaving an airport. She took out her compact mirror and hoped she'd look like that when she landed.

Suddenly the engine started and the butterflies in her stomach began fluttering. This was the beginning of her jet-set life.

1967

Anita Pallenberg decided to leave her boyfriend behind and travel to Morocco with the rest of the Rolling Stones boys. Her boyfriend, Brian had fallen sick and he had urged her to continue the trip without him. So she left, continuing on her holiday. And if she had been completely honest with herself, he had been getting on her nerves anyway.

She loved Morocco. The air was full of clouds of smoke and the echoes of calls to prayer. The sun had turned her skin a dark caramel brown and freckled her nose. The atmosphere was so soothing that she relaxed and thought everyone seemed so much more relaxed too.

The Rolling Stones boys were facing a media storm back home in London. They had recently been caught throwing a house party with a lot of drugs in their possession. So they decided to come to Marrakesh to get away for awhile before facing the music.

One evening while sitting in a local cafe, they began to discuss whether they might end up in prison. They seemed calm but annoyed at the drug bust. They wondered whether someone might have tipped the fuzz off.

After several discussions over shishas and green teas, Anita got up from the table.

"Where are you going?" Keith said from a cloud of smoke.

"Shopping. They have a market right around the corner."

"I'll come with you."

They walked together through the market. Anita eyed up all the amazing textiles and local fashions. She picked up a tunic and a floor-length dress in a pattern she had never seen before. Clothes from Africa, India and East Asia had started to show up in the boutiques back home, so she didn't worry about looking out of place on the streets of London. Her style was slowly moving away from mod to something a little more bohemian.

While she was bartering with a local stall owner, she eyed Keith standing in his loud-coloured blazer, messy thick hair and shades. He looked completely out of place in Marrakesh, she chuckled. But she thought he was kind for escorting her around the market and wondered if her boyfriend Brian would do the same. She tutted to herself as she remembered Brian's love for drugs and how he would probably be on them right now if he were here. She was secretly glad that she was now standing here with Keith and not Brian.

1968

Kate was very proud of her hand-painted sign. She had used many bright coloured paints, pressed flowers and a touch of glitter for that extra jazz. She held it up high as she walked among the protesters in Trafalgar Square. She had secretly skipped school to be there.

It was things like this that would compel her mother to ask if she was one of those 'hipsters'. They were called hippies for short. You could spot one by their long unstyled hair, their casual clothes and a general chilled out aura. But her mother thought they were stoners with terrible hair.

So she replied no because she'd rather not let her worry. But she was a part of a small hippie community in her school. They believed in peace and love. Kate couldn't help but become a part of the love revolution. Which is how she found herself at the anti-Vietnam protest.

For the day, she wore her floor-length kimono with a maxi skirt she'd found at a charity shop. And she wore a necklace that she handmade herself from small bits of metal that she found. As she looked around the protest, a lot of the women had a similar style. These were her people. And if only her mother could see beyond the drugs, she'd understand.

Kate gasped as a nearby police officer started beating one of her classmates with a bat. Another girl next to her started screaming although it was unclear if it was because of the police brutality or the LSD she had just taken. Either way Kate backed away from the scene enraged. This was meant to be a peaceful protest and was shocked that the very people that are paid to protect her, were now beating her non-violent friends to the ground.

As another one of her friends hit the pavement next to her, appearing to have been flung by a policeman, Kate picked up a rock and threw it straight at the policeman's balls.

1969

It was nearing the end of the sixties and Mary was feeling a little deflated. She had been glued to her transistor all night, listening to Radio Caroline. Two of her favourite bands were in turmoil. The Beatles were rumoured to be splitting up and Rolling Stone Brian Jones had just died. Mary was worried about what the future would hold.

A couple of days later, the Rolling Stones held a free concert in Hyde Park in memory of Brian. Mary headed there as soon as it was daylight, thinking she'd be early but found so many fans were already there with candles. She joined them in a song and talked about all her favourite songs. She danced, made flower crowns and received many compliments on her hotpants until it was time for the Stones to take to the stage.

Mick Jagger read a eulogy and white butterflies flew from the stage. It was so beautiful that she cried. Through her tears, she looked around at the sad faces beside her. There was a woman in a dark top and capri trouser, mascara smudged from crying. There was a woman in smart trousers and a blouse, keenly jotting things down in a notebook. To her left was a girl with a sharp cut bob and a shift dress hugging her friend in a miniskirt. There were two friends to her right, consoling each other too. One was wearing a Moroccan tunic and the other in a turquoise Pucci maxi dress. As she watched a Hells Angel casually walk by, she felt an arm wrap around her shoulder.

"You alright there sister?" It was a long-haired girl in jeans and a white fringed top that was so translucent that you could see she wasn't wearing a bra. "You look like you could use a friend?"

The girl offered Mary an oversized cigarette that smelled like armpit. She gratefully took the cigarette, had a big drag of it and felt a calm wash over her as The Stones began playing another song.

Suddenly she wasn't that worried about the future anymore. Now women could wear whatever they wanted. Shorts, trousers, miniskirts, no bras, no corsets. Just like those white butterflies, they were free.

4. Signature Sixties Looks

Even though the sixties made it socially acceptable to wear short skirts, hot pants and pretty much everything that we wear now, some key looks and pieces were unique to the decade.

The Beatnik Look

The Beatniks would meet in late-night cafes, listening to bebop jazz and reciting dirty poetry. In popular media, the beatniks wore berets while smoking hand-rolled cigarettes from behind their horn-rimmed glasses. They also smoked marijuana which made them seem edgy and interesting at a time when most people had never seen drugs before. On the record player would be Dizzy Gillespie or Miles Davis, and on the bookshelf were the immortal words of Allen Ginsberg and Jack Kerouac.

As the beatniks gathered more recruits, the media began to satirise them into something more pretentious. They gave beatniks superficial traits and focused on their pseudo-intellectualism. The all-black clothing and berets became a uniform.

But the Beats weren't all about wearing black and writing drunk poetry. Their philosophy was that they should all work on themselves from the inside rather than worry about external things. They were about rejecting consumerism.

This mildly explains their minimalist style. The girls wore their hair flat to rebel against beauty salons and they had minimal clothing to reject the middle-class fashions. They wouldn't dare wear designer labels or any labels at all for that matter. It was mainly plain capris with a shirt or jumper. Gillian Hills immortalised the look in the film Beat Girl.

The Mod Look

If you were to pick up a 1960s costume from a fancy dress shop, it would most likely be a mod outfit. I can imagine it would be a black and white dress with a matching baker boy hat and white boots. But the mod style was so much more than just this one look.

Mods were the most fashion-forward women of the sixties. These fashionistas were branded 'The Modernists' (Mods for short).

Taking inspiration from the beatniks, mods hung out in coffee bars while smoking and listening to music. It was a very social affair that involved conversations about French cinema and R&B whilst on amphetamines.

Modernist men could easily be spotted. Most travelled on their Vespas with their Crombie coats flailing behind them. They would wear a well-tailored suit or a v-neck jumper paired with a button-down Ben Sherman shirt.

Women, however, wore the latest trends including mini skirts and A-line dresses. The modern woman's look was mainly influenced by London's street style and French New Wave movies. A lot of women dressed androgynously with short hair like Jean Seberg. But others wore their hair long and backcombed like Dusty Springfield.

Hiroku Matusmoto in dressed in typical Mod fashion

One of the key outfits were shift dresses, coloured tights and dolly shoes. They loved geometric, Mondrian and bold patterns. They were into the latest trends, and they set them.

The Dolly Girl Look

"Dolly" is a sixties fashion trend that not just anyone can pull off. If you do it wrong, you'll end up attracting the kind of men who own vans and stock sweets in their back pocket. Why? Because the "dolly girl" look was completely inspired by little girls.

But not teenage girls that knock around with their short skirts and too much impulse spray. Not even the nine-year-olds who wear Barbie tops and plastic sunglasses. Even younger. But somehow, the sixties made looking like you still shit your pants seem very chic.

The white tights, the school shoes and the girly patterned baby doll dress. This is one of the most typical looks of Dolly Girl fashion; dress like a little girl but still look like a stylish adult woman.

The dolly girl look was a style that a lot of the mods were into. They wore heavy makeup to exaggerate their Bambi eyes. They'd pair that with gingham or crochet dresses and make sure it was short. They'd take a leaf out of the school girl's book and pull out those knee-high socks and pigtails. Pretty much, anything a little girl would wear.

Pattie Boyd dressed in Dolly Girl Style, Vogue 1967

Peter Pan Collared Dresses

When Roman Polanski released his film adaptation of *Rosemary's Baby*, he was intending to scare audiences. Well, he did do that. But he also sparked off a fashion trend. His leading lady wore several peter pan collared dresses paired with her short pixie hair cut. Although white tab collared dresses had been around way before 1968, Mia had helped it become an iconic sixties look.

The Beehive

The sixties was where it all began. The fez-inspired pillbox hats were hugely popular at the time with America's sweetheart Jackie Kennedy being a huge advocate.

Hairdresser Margaret Vinci Heldt adored the fez and wanted to create a hairstyle that could slot right into one. So, she created a huge backcombed bouffant which was two parts hair, one part face and showered in hairspray. When her style was photo-ready, she decorated the look with a small bee pin. The look was published in Modern Beauty Shop Magazine and it didn't take long before a writer dubbed it "the beehive".

The Ronettes became huge fans and made light-blocking hair their trademark. Many more celebrities, from Brigitte Bardot to Audrey Hepburn, adopted the beehive too and it became one of the most popular hairstyles of the era.

The Ronettes rocking their beehives

The Space Age Look

At that time, the race to Space was happening. Russia and the US competed to be the first to land on the moon. The sudden focus on Space, rocket ships and astronauts began to influence fashion design. Suddenly women were wearing shiny silver dresses, big avant-garde hats and plastic shoes. It was the sixties version of future fashion. It's probably ironic that now, in the future, you're reading a book on how to dress like it's the sixties.

The Jet Set

The economy was thriving and a lot of women were now getting a share of the money. And with airline prices being more affordable, rich women were flying all over the world in search of the next party.

These aristocrats and celebrities were called the jet setters and their look was immortalised through Emilio Pucci's luxury loungewear. Palazzo pants, maxi dresses and silk scarfs were their key pieces. And they were all decorated in Pucci's staple geometric pattern.

The Hippie Look

LSD, cannabis and peyote were on the menu in the sixties. It caused excessive creativity and was allowing people to think more about the world that they live in. But most dangerously of all, it brought people together in celebration of peace and freedom from conformity. How terrible.

The psychedelic drugs caused young people to pick some "far out" clothing. They wore loose-fitted material, ash-stained denim and stolen garden flowers. They didn't cut their hair (especially the boys) and took a lot of influence from Eastern culture including their clothes.

Of course not all hippies took drugs, but they did have a common concern for the environment. Which is why it was the beginning of the vintage and recycled clothes industry.

Wearing second hand clothes lead to a lot of different hippie looks. There was the more traditional jeans and top variety like Janis Joplin, a more bohemian look like Anita Pallenberg or a more medieval, witchy style like the band Coven. And when thousands flocked together to festivals to listen to psychedelic music, indulge in psychedelic drugs and dance like an inflatable wobbly man, the festival look was born.

The hippie style in England

Nightwear

Although fashion was changing, what women wore at home didn't evolve over the decade. By 1969, most women were wearing the same style nightwear that they were in the fifties. But if you want to recreate a sixties lounge look at home, we better look at the key pieces.

Baby Doll Dresses

This style of dress has a super flattering silhouette for any body type and it's so floaty that it will make you feel like you're in *Valley Of The Dolls*. If you throw on a pair of white tights, you can wear it outside too if you're going for that dolly girl look.

Matching Sets

Taffeta trousers paired with matching warm knitted tops were super groovy to wear at home during this time. There isn't much difference between these and pyjamas except they're not made for sleeping in.

Maxi Dresses

Sometimes the sixties floor-length lounge dresses that you'll come across in vintage shops, look good enough to wear to prom. This was because a lot of wealthier women would wear them for entertaining guests at home. Who wouldn't like waltzing around at home in a fancy dress and a glass of wine?

Gowns

Dressing gowns will be around longer than cockroaches because they're so useful. A gown can spice up any loungewear,

Sharon Tate wearing a typical sixties night dress

make life warmer or can be quickly thrown on to answer the door, if you like to lounge around in nothing at all.

Pyjamas

The trend of matching pyjama sets is still going strong. But in the sixties, they made the cutest style of pyjamas in the form of little peek-a-boo frilly short sets.

Kaftans

Towards the end of the sixties a lot of fashion was inspired by Eastern dress. This is why the Kaftan popped up in the loungewear section of a woman's wardrobe. It was the perfect piece to be comfortable and look luxurious at the same time.

Slip Dresses

I do love a good slip. Slips were traditionally worn as undergarments. In the sixties, it became more acceptable to lounge around the house in one. Although you wouldn't be caught outside in one. That wasn't acceptable until the '90s.

House Coats

You don't see these anymore. House coats were worn during the colder months at home. They often came in soft, thick fabric and sometimes quilted like a blanket. I hope they make a comeback.

5. Style Icons

Attitudes to women's fashion were changing so rapidly in the sixties. It was hard for a lot of girls to understand what was acceptable to wear and what would get them thrown in prison. They needed someone to guide them, to show them what they could get away with wearing and what their friends would think was cool. They needed a style icon.

There were a lot of fashion forward women in the sixties that didn't care about what was acceptable to most tastes. And they had the power of celebrity behind them. They helped introduce new looks and pieces to the rest of the western world and make it more accessible to other women. Without these women, maybe the miniskirt wouldn't have taken off and we'd still be in stockings.

These are the women that made sixties fashion their own, and in turn created sixties fashion. These are the women we need to celebrate.

Audrey Hepburn's street style

Audrey Hepburn

From the moment Audrey Hepburn stepped out of a cab in Breakfast At Tiffany's, she confirmed her role as a style icon. Sixties girls across the world began looking for a little black dress like her character's Holly Golightly.

Previously, she had appeared in fashionable movies in the fifties like *Funny Face* and *Sabrina*. But it wasn't until she popped on her Givenchy black dress and munched on a pastry outside Tiffany's jewelry store that we fell in love forever. The look has been referenced in *Gossip Girl*, *Sex and The City* and so much more.

Audrey went on to star in many fashionable roles throughout the sixties and even off-camera, she always looked perfectly polished.

Jackie Kennedy

America's first lady, Jackie Kennedy, became an icon to housewives across the world. Her style was modest, but always on trend. She had a love for French fashion and often commissioned versions of the latest French styles to be made for her.

She was a model wife, fashionable and made her president husband happy. Although she did once said, "Sex is a bad thing because it rumples the clothes." The perfect modest statement that had conservative women applauding. But I'm not sure how happy that made her randy husband.

Jackie Kennedy wearing an on-trend leopard print coat

Twiggy 1967, By Lewis Morely

Twiggy

When Twiggy had all her hair chopped off, little did she know that it would be the best thing she ever did. From the salon, she was scouted and went on to become the face of the sixties. She still is one of the most recognisable faces today. Her big cartoon eyes and twig-like legs became one of the most popular looks of the decade. She even started her own fashion line and released crochet patterns for fashion fans to make at home.

Britt Ekland's style was copied by girls everywhere

Britt Ekland

Britt was a Swedish girl who grew up thinking she was fat and ugly. One day, on a trip to Italy, whilst sampling the local coffee she met a talent agent who saw potential in her. He offered for her to come to London to audition for films. Britt accepted and soon scored small roles and a famous English husband Peter Sellers.

Her style was very innocent looking with pastels, her signature bows and cardigans. She did the dolly look very well, but occasionally mixed it up with a more grown up suit. But never forgetting the bow.

Ann Karina's Sailor Outfit in 'Femme Est Une Femme', Pathé
Contemporary Films/Photofest

Anna Karina

Anna was originally from Denmark, but the French adopted her as one of their own. She became iconic for appearing in poetic French New Wave movies with a blunt brunette bob and a cheeky smile. She made style history when she wore a sailor dress in the film *Femme Est Une Femme*. Shortly after, sailor-style designs became a key look in mod French fashion.

Brigitte Bardot's Street Style

Brigitte Bardot

Bardot began the decade with being a fashionista after having success in many French movies in the 1950s. During that time, she made the bikini popular and made gingham the hottest pattern around when she wore it for her wedding dress. It even inspired a sixties boutiques to use the pattern which brought them an abundance of fame (Biba btw).

Her style evolved from fifties darling to sixties French chic to seventies bohemian by the end of the era and she rocked them all. She was very daring with her clothes and often took risks that many conservative people were shocked by. But she wore what she wanted and even got naked, regardless of what people thought of her.

One of her signature looks was her big blonde messy beehive which she wore during the day and night. And she paired it with thick black eyeliner.

Catherine Deneuve

This French goddess dazzled in the raunchy flick *Belle Du Jour*. She played the part of a dutiful wife who worked as a sex worker during the day to fulfil her sexual desires. When she was wearing clothes, she was beautifully dressed by Yves Saint Laurent. Off-screen she dressed incredibly well too. She dressed very 'French Mod'; a bit of a London mod style mixed with that Parisian cool. She'd wear berets, chequered shirts and bows in her blonde hair which was always beautifully combed out of her face.

Catherine Denuve's minimalist style in 1968

Hiroku Matsumoto

Hiroku was a Japanese model who became Pierre Cardin's muse. He fell in love with her on a visit to Japan in 1960. From then, she would eventually follow him back to France where she would become the first Japanese model for a French clothing company.

Her style was adored by the French fashion world and she promptly began appearing in many magazines. She became known for having a blunt bob and short skirts which gave her the ultimate 'mod' aesthetic.

Hiroku Matsumoto (on ladder) for Pierre Cardin, 1966

Helen Gurley Brown

Helen rose to fame by writing 'Sex & The Single Girl'- a controversial book about getting a career and getting laid. Shortly after, she found herself in charge of Cosmopolitan magazine and became an icon for career girls everywhere.

Eunice W Johnson

Eunice was a rock star when it came to fashion. She prompted make-up companies to cater to darker-skinned women and was the creator and founder of Ebony magazine. She was an first-rate entrepreneur and the first African-American woman to have a Picasso painting in her home.

Edie Sedwick (centre) in Andy Warhol's film Afternoon

Edie Sedgwick

Edie was an artist herself who, one fateful night, met artist Andy Warhol and the rest was history. Together they were inseparable. He took her to every event he went to and featured her in a lot of his films. Edie died her hair silver to match his.

Andy Warhol's studio was dubbed the factory, and it became the hottest place to be in New York. Eventually Vogue was interested and used Edie as a model. Her statement style became black tights and a top. She'd throw over a huge mink coat and some chandelier earrings.

To this day she remains a style icon. Her style was perfectly captured in the biopic *Factory Girl* starring Sienna Miller.

Nico's androdgynous style in New York 1965 By Steve Schapiro

Nico

After underground cinema, Andy Warhol's decided his next project was music. He was introduced to the band Velvet Underground and fell in love with their strange, new sound.

Shortly after, Andy met singer Nico eating fruit out of her jug of wine and decided to bring her along for the ride. He was enamoured with her deep, moody voice and Viking-esque look. She wore mod clothes that verged on androdgynous.

Eventually, Nico went solo again and moved on from the Factory scene and decided to dye her trademark blonde hair dark. To reflect her new music, she began wearing witchy-like clothes and was one of the first to have a 'gothic' style.

Peggy Moffit

Peggy Moffit was a model who was completely ahead of her time. She wore modern fashion in a way that was never worn before and broke conventions of what a model should look like. Her style was futuristic and avante garde way before Lady Gaga was born.

Her trademark was her mime-style makeup that was always painted black and white. That bob was cut by iconic hairdresser Vidal Sassoon and was called the 'five point'. One of her most iconic looks was when she wore the topless bikini designed by Rudi Gernreich called the 'Monokini'. A lot of models refused to wear it, but Peggy stepped up to the plate and was photographed wearing one of the most controversial designs of the sixties.

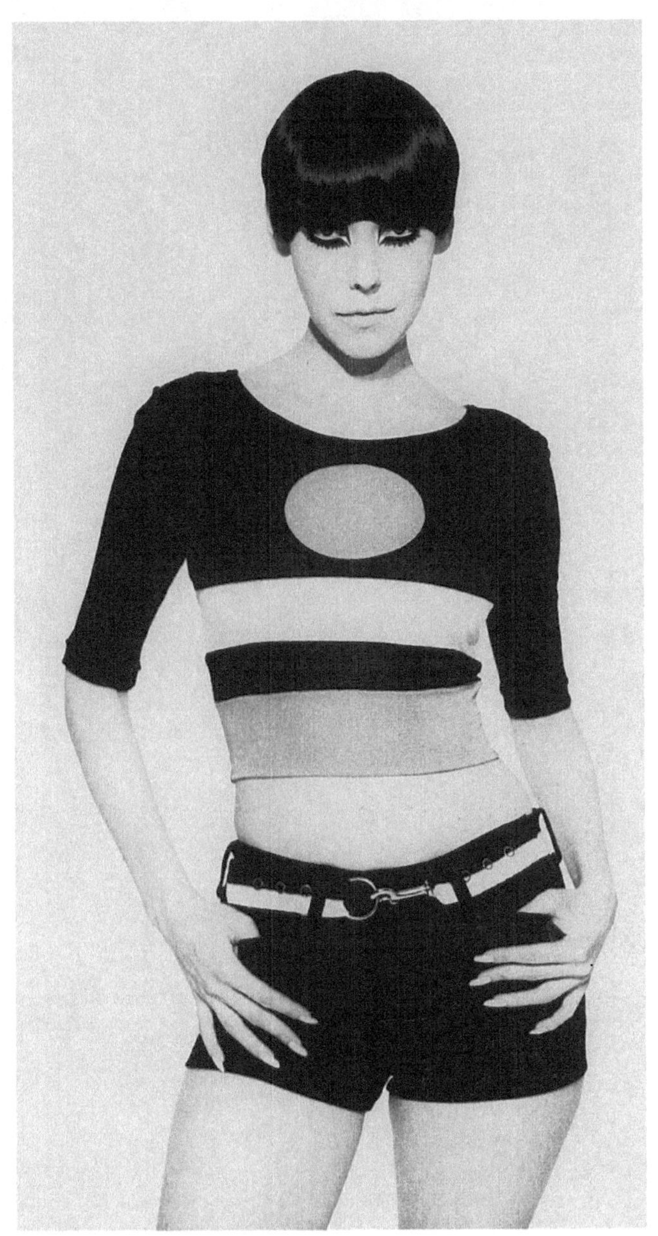

Peggy Moffit's futuristic style and trademark makeup

Donyale Luna in a fashion show

Donyale Luna

In March 1966 Donyale Luna became the first black cover girl for British Vogue (and any other Vogue for that matter). She became an inspiration for black girls everywhere who were tired of only seeing white faces in the magazines that they couldn't relate to.

Donyale also had impecable taste. She adored the surreal and the avant-garde. She made contact lenses her thing changed her eye colour depending on the mood.

Although she was faced with a lot of racial discrimination, she never let it hold her back from being the queen of modelling.

Sophia by Beaumont Nathan

Sophia Loren

Sophia began her acting career at the age of 16 and went on to be the first actress to win an Oscar for a foreign-language performance. Throughout the fifties and sixties she became the vision of Italian beauty. She favoured dresses that accentuated her hourglass figure and big hair to match her big hazel eyes.

But she did more than just influence women with her style. She championed fuller, thicker figures like her own. She always claimed she'd never go on a diet and everything you see she "owes to spaghetti".

Virna Lisi during the filming of 'The Heist' 1969

Virna Lisi

Another actress from Italy (they have all the glamour in that country) was making a lot of waves across the world. Virna Lisi was listed to be the Italian Marilyn Monroe but she had sixties flair. Her eyes were framed with slick black eyeline like cat eyes. It wasn't long before Hollywood came sniffing.

Francoise Hardy

Francoise was the face of French Yé-yé music and sold records all across the world. Her style was always classic French and very androgynous. She liked to wear suits and trousers, but quite often mixed it up with the occasional Paco Rabanne dress. She always wore her hair flat and her make up minimal.

Anita Pallenberg

Anita was better known for being the girlfriend of Rolling Stone, Keith Richards. But she was more than just a groupie, she was a queen of bohemian fashion and a great actress. She had a passion for frilly collars, floppy hats and kimonos. Her fashion influence came from her travels across the world, picking up tunics and traditional dress wherever she went. Even Keith acredits his rock n roll style to Anita, whose clothes he wore when he was to lazy to find his own.

Jayne Mansfield

There were some women who still adored the glamour of fifties Hollywood and for that, they had Jayne Mansfield. Although she was dubbed the working man's Marilyn, she had her own unique spin on everything she did.

She used her clothes to make headlines. There were several wardrobe malfunctions and a lot of pink. By the sixties, she began to embrace the new styles and attitudes. She grew her hair out longer, pinned it with a bow and carried a little dog with her everywhere she went.

Jayne Mansfield's sixties style & her little dog

Jane Birkin with her famous basket bag

Jane Birkin

Jane Birkin left England to live in Paris without knowing a word of French. And rather than ending up on the streets, Paris adopted her as one of their own (seriously, can Paris adopt me too?).

She was quickly scouted as a model and she took up acting auditions. When she began to appear in moves, it wasn't her costumes that grabbed the fashion world's attention. It was her off duty style. She was snapped all over the city with her tomboy denim jeans, plain white tops and a basket bag. This look became so iconic they named the Birkin bag after her.

Angela Davis

Angela Davis always stood up for what she believed in and always looked effortlessly chic when doing it. The most important thing about Angela, is that she made an impact on equality for black people in America.

But her style can also be considered important. Many black women before the late sixties had been more comfortable wearing wigs to make their hair seem straighter. Thankfully women like Angela wore their natural hair proudly and paved the way for other women to do the same.

Janis Joplin

Janis had a powerful voice that could drive a festival audience crazy. It was husky, loud and raw. It was hard to believe it came from this petite girl from Texas.

Her style was mainly influenced by the Haight-Ashbury crowd that consisted of flower children and drop outs. She wore baggy clothes, an excessive amount of beads and flares. When she was at the height of her fame, she decided to make wearing feather boas in her hair, her thing.

Angela Davis being interviewed

Janis Joplin 1968, Jim Marshall

Uschi Obermaier by German Mehner

Uschi Obermaier

Uschi was a German model who found herself at the heart of the sexual revolution. She lived in a commune with a writer. Together they attended festivals, protests and celebrated free love. She became the poster girl for the counter culture and even had an influence on John Lennon. Her loved to wear head bands and fringing. Everything was worn with her hair wild and chilled out attitude.

Diana Vreeland

Diana took the reigns of American Vogue in the sixties and made a huge statement by turning a stuffy high fashion magazine into a young girl's bible featuring musicians, actresses and anything new that was going on at the time. While her magazine was full of diverse and modern fashion, she knew a career girl had to keep her wardrobe functional. She kept her own style simple by wearing similar clothes every day, with a splash of her favourite rogue.

Pattie Boyd

The Beatles were one of the most popular bands in the world. So naturally, when one of the band started dating model Pattie Boyd, girls wanted to be like her. Pattie's personal style evolved over the decade from mod dolly girl to festival glam in paisley dresses and long flowing hair.

6. Labels

A lot of girls in the sixties were handy with a thread and needle. They'd flick through their magazine and recreated the styles. Their homemade dresses were completely customised to their body and tastes. Even the highest paid supermodel Jean Shrimpton made her own dresses... with her own dress maker.

But what about the women who couldn't sew or had no time to? Where did they get their clothes? We know some looks, trends and who was wearing the clothes but if we truly want to explore sixties fashion, we need to look at their sources.

Boutiques

When they weren't hand making the pieces themselves (or getting their mum to make it), they were buying it at boutique stores. London boutiques, in particular, became world-famous for selling the most on-trend clothes of the era.

Biba boutique, London

Biba

Biba designer Barbara Hulanicki once said that her ideal customers were "postwar babies who had been deprived of nourishing protein in childhood and grew up into beautiful skinny people: a designer's dream. I didn't take much of them to look outstanding."

She opened her first little shop in Kensington in 1964 after running a successful mail-order boutique. Biba was so sought-after that it quickly expanded, eventualy becoming a department store that made their own make-up, accessories and baked beans!

At the time, Biba's clothes were something that you could wear today, and buy a new one tomorrow. Now, they've become vintage collector's pieces... even the baked beans.

The Biba look was soft and feminine. Designer and founder Barbara Hulanicki took a lot of influence from the 1920s Art Nouveau and Art Deco styles, and it reflected in her designs- especially the eveningwear.

Key staples of Biba's look included droopy low cut necklines with ties, head-to-toe prints, bias-cut maxi dresses, midi length double-breasted trench coats and long rows of buttons. Biba also used gathered in sleeves with long cuffs, flared skirts and long-line waistcoats that cut off at the same length as a mini skirt. Biba popularised the maxi coat which is one of my favourite pieces. And by the 1970s, leopard print was a heavy feature along with fake fur collars and shrugs.

Biba has been revived several times, most recently by House Of Fraser. They may have bought the name, but they certainly can't buy style.

Mary (top) with Alexander and models, 1966, National Portrait Gallery London

Bazaar

The Bazaar boutique was home to many beautiful trendy designs by Mary Quant. She made mini skirts, hot pants, coloured tights and even duvets popular. To get people interested in her boutique, she'd turn the music up loud, offer free drinks and make witty little window displays. She sounds like my kind of woman.

Bazaar became the place to be seen in London and her clothes were the things to be seen in. She was a trendsetter and became a national treasure.

But since she sold the rights to her brand in 2000, there's been a lot of confusion about what is an original and what is a reproduction. But a few things can distinguish the two.

Mary was influenced by mods and dancers. She loved the city-dwelling beatniks and the youthful glow that began bursting from the streets during the sixties. It was her customers who inspired her. The active, interesting and on-trend teenagers that would wander down the streets of Chelsea looking for a cute dress and a happening to wear it to.

Her most famous look was her jersey dress. It was the perfect material to use for chilly England – thick and stretchy. Her dresses often came in a shift style or with a drop-down waist. She also began to make onesies, hot pants and tops in the fabric.

Later on down the line, she began to have fun with PVC and made a wet look collection. Shoes and coats were made from PVC and had a modern, futuristic look about them that she adored. She even made a dress out of paper (you probably wouldn't find that on the vintage market today though).

White dagger collars were her thing as well as a ring pull zip down the front of a dress. She also helped to make trousers fashionable for women including dungarees. Though she made many trousers, they've become a rare find on the vintage circuit.

Al Radley with one of his pieces in 1968, Bryan Wharton

Radley

Alfred Radley began his clothing manufacturing company in the sixties. Eventually, he expanded his business and took over the Quorum boutique. Acquiring a very sought after swinging London designer - Ossie Clark. Ossie Clark had a unique style that could only be described as 'folk princess'. He often created maxi dresses with a whole range of colour. From the bright and bold to the wispy, pastel colours. One key element of his designs were Celia Birtwell's patterns which were floral, pretty and occasionally trippy.

He used a lot of crepe and silk for the dresses. Satin appeared a lot too, and even with the trousers. They tried to use any material that was light and flowy. This was a look for the jet setters and the bohemians.

Granny Takes A Trip

Sheila Cohen and her boyfriend Nigel Weymouth began their boutique together in Kings Road. Sheila was a huge collector of vintage clothes, especially Victorian and oriental clothes. She began to sell them in the boutique with a twist. She'd customise them into modern styles and add her little quirks. Just like Granny's clothes had taken a trip.

The boutique became well known for its double-breasted jackets and suits. They were often inspired by art, using William Morris patterns and floral print on their jackets. These pieces attracted the attention of The Beatles and Jimi Hendrix who bagged their own William Morris jackets.

The clothes reflected the world of hippies and psychedelics which is what the shop became known for. But Nigel had other ideas. He saw himself as more of a mod and he designed the interiors to reflect that. Eventually, this is the disagreement that led Nigel and Sheila to sell the boutique at the end of the sixties.

Hendrix in a Granny Takes A Trip Blazer

Foale and Tuffin by Richard Lester

Foale and Tuffin

Marion Foale and Sally Tuffin graduated art college in 1961 and decided together what they wanted to do next- start a business without the help of a man. They began to design clothes that they thought were fun and playful. By 1962 one of their designs was featured in Vogue and by the next year, they had succeeded.

These women helped pioneer the look of the Mod girls that rambled about on the streets of London. They used what they dubbed 'granny fabrics' like lace, corduroy and organza. But they always looked modern when they were cut into the sixties silhouettes with chequers and geometric patterns.

A-line dresses, clean-cut suits and sharp tailoring became their look. As the sixties rolled on their clothes became more relaxed, but their most iconic work lives on in their skirt suits and shift dresses.

Tuffin once said their clothes were for "girls who needed to express themselves. They were young, busy, trendy, wanting to do their own thing and kick down the barriers of so many years. These girls wanted to hoick up their skirts – literally – and get rid of their suspenders."

Other Boutiques

Here's a list of some other boutique names worthy of a lookout:

- Annacat
- Apple
- Bill Gibb
- Blanes
- Bus Stop
- Carnegie Of London
- Clobber
- Diana Warren
- Dollyrockers
- Elsie Whiteley
- Frank Usher
- Frederick Starke
- Gerald McCann
- Gina Fratini
- Hardy Amies
- Harella
- Horrockses
- Janice Wainwright
- Jean Allen
- Jean Varon
- Jeff Banks
- John Bates
- John Charles
- John Stephen
- Laura Ashley
- Lord Kitcheners
- Marion Donaldson
- Marshall & Snellgrove
- Norman Hartnell
- Origin
- Quad
- Quorum
- Ricci Michaels
- Robert Dorland
- Samuel Sherman
- Shubette
- Susan Small
- St Michael
- Sybil Connolly
- The White House
- Twiggy
- Victor Stiebel
- Windsmoor

A-Z Of Sixties Designers

Although teenagers were influencing fashion, designers still had their place in the world. And if you want to be able to spot some of the clothes of the era, it's helpful to get to know the designers that created some of the most iconic looks of the time that filtered down to high street.

My advice would be to pick your favourite designer from this list and get to know their work. Have a look at old photos and study the details of that designer. The more familiar you become with one designer the easier it will be to spot an original or a sixties high street version. Often boutiques copied a designer's work or the occasional girl grabbed a needle and sewed her own version. But designer or replica, either way, it's still fabulous.

André Corréges futuristic design, 1960s

André Corrèges

This French fashion designer had a passion for art and clothes. But his father had other plans. He wanted him to be an engineer. So Andrew went to engineering school, but the moment he left, he went to Paris and worked in fashion.

By 1961, he launched his first collection which began his influence on the fashion world. He is known to be one of the designers who invented the mini skirt and revolutionised fashion.

His designs were geometrical, simple but extremely well made. He became known for his 'little white dress' and a low heeled white ankle boot that became the gogo boot. The boot of the sixties.

He also dipped his toes in for the Space Age look, for his 1964 collection. That year, he was praised for using materials like plastic and PVC which was unusual for a couturier.

Balenciaga sack dress, 1959

Balenciaga

Near the end of the fifties, Christóbel Balenciaga showcased his sack dress to the world. It was a dress that went straight up and down, with no definition at the waist. It wasn't well-received at the time but a couple of years later his sack dress would be noted as the beginning of the shift silhouette. He continued to innovate with fashion throughout the sixties, creating babydoll shapes and using his Spanish influences. But sadly in 1968, he shut up his fashion house and passed away a few years later.

Chanel Suit & Bag, 1960

Chanel

Coco Chanel returned to France in the 1950s after being exiled to Switzerland for several years. When she returned she was appalled to find that the restrictive, uber-feminine looks she campaigned against in the 1920s, had returned. Fashion was celebrating tiny waists, big full skirts and housewives again.

She quickly pulled out her rolls of tweed and set to work. She reopened the House Of Chanel and put her clothes back in the spotlight. This time, she threw in bags, jewellery and more perfume into the mix.

Her suits were the most popular. They were made in tweed and framed with a pattern around the edgings. The skirts were just below the knee and came in shades of sherbert pink and cream. She'd also wrap the designs in houndstooth too.

Chanel would go on to design air hostess outfits throughout most of the sixties and begin conjuring up evening gowns that were extravagant but still looked comfortable. But the most easily recognisable trait of Chanel is the tweed suit. It was adored by career girls in the sixties who now could afford it with their own money.

Jean Shrimpton in Chloe 1967, David Bailey

Chloé

Chloé was founded in 1952 and offered luxury ready to wear clothes for the lady who had money but no time for a fitting. By the sixties, Chloé was creating shirt dresses and silk blouses. The fashion house's style became carefree, romantic and fun. In the mid-sixties, a young Karl Lagerfeld joined Chloe and created a hand-painted floor length casual dress which added a little bohemian flair to the brand. By 1969, Chloe released their silk trousers and became the master of laid back elegance.

Christian Dior Dress 1968

Dior

At the end of the fifties, the house of Dior ousted its head designer Yves Saint Laurent in favour of a more conservative designer. They continued to create the Dior style with a nipped-in waist and longer hemlines despite the ongoing fashion revolution. But they did modernise a little during that time. In 1967, they released a ready to wear range called Miss Dior for the women who couldn't afford couture.

Audrey in her Breakfast At Tiffany's Dress By Givenchy 1961

Givenchy

Hubert de Givenchy made fashion history when he designed the first shirt dress in the 1950s. But when he met Audrey Hepburn, he became legendary.

The pair partnered up for several of her movies and, most famously, *Breakfast At Tiffanys* in 1961. He designed for her the little black dress that became the most talked-about dress in movie history. It flattered her tiny frame perfectly and she wore it with such sass.

Givenchy's dresses were mostly long, elegant pieces that cinched in at the waist. Unlike Chanel, he promoted the femininity of a woman and drew attention to the hourglass figure.

Penelope Tree in an Ungaro suit 1968, Richard Avedon

Emanuel Ungaro

Emanuel Ungaro studied under the Balenciaga fashion house before opening up his own in 1965. He wasn't shy with his first designs. He was immediately innovating using unusual shapes and embellishments. But what stood out most about his designs, was his use of loud, flamboyant patterns including this bold chequered suit as modelled by Penelope Tree.

Emilio Pucci's collection of jumpsuits and dresses

Emilio Pucci

Emilio Pucci first began by designing ski wear and was one of the first to make a one-piece ski suit. He continued with his love of geometrical and kaleidoscope patterns and began to print them on scarves and blouses.

By the sixties, his designs were worn by Marilyn Monroe, Jackie Kennedy and Sophia Loren. His clothes can mostly be spotted by the patterns and colours of silk blouses, loose trousers and scarves. It was psychedelic luxury.

Fendi Fur Coat 1965

Fendi

In 1965, Fendi roped in young designer Karl Lagerfeld (he was a busy boy) who began working with leathers and innovating the brand's designs. It wasn't long before the fashion house put him in charge of their fur range. From then on, Karl would design for Fendi up until his death.

Guy Laroche coat and trouser set 1965

Guy Laroche

Guy Laroche began his first ready to wear collection in 1961 and brought his bold, bright colour palette to the fashion world. His designs reflected the times with it's loud colours and patterns like this matching set in 1965. He used cut out shapes, minidresses and fringing.

Krizia dress in Milan, Giorgio Casali

Krizia

Mariuccia Mandelli was an experimental designer and if she decided to make her creations anytime before the sixties, she probably would have been laughed out of the fashion world. She'd use unconventional materials like eel skins or cork for her designs and crafted them into unusual shapes. In 1964, she presented a completely black and white collection for which she won an award. She was truly ahead of her time.

Louis Féraud designs 1969

Louis Féraud

Louis Féraud loved making wearable fashion rather than fashion for art. During the sixties, he'd fall in love with the a-line shape that was popular with his younger clientele. He crafted simple but well-crafted designs for the wealthy mod woman.

Missoni knitwear playsuits

Missoni

An Italian couple began their knitwear business in the fifties and had a love for colour. Gradually, their clientele grew and Missoni flourised into a popular brand by the sixties. They began doing things with knitwear that had never been done before. They made suits, eveningwear and two pieces from something that was originally reserved for jumpers. However, it was their use of bold patterns and colour that became synonymous with the style of the decade.

Oscar De La Renta with a late sixties design, Oscar De La Renta

Oscar De La Renta

In 1965, Oscar De La Renta set up his own fashion company in New York. He began designing for society ladies, many of whom were friends with his French Vogue editor wife. But it wasn't until he began designing gipsy-inspired designs in the late sixties that he became popular with a younger audience. He went from dressing the convservative Jackie Kennedy to Cher.

Paco Rabanne and his designs during the film set of Casino Royale

Paco Rabanne

This Spanish designer opened his fashion house in 1966 and blew the fashion world by using unconventional materials like paper, plastic, and metal. His most famous design is the disc dress which can be seen on Audrey Hepburn in *Two For The Road*. It's glamourous, fun and expensive-looking all at the same time. For this reason, you can find a lot of sixties dresses in this style, a lot of women handmade them.

He was also forward thinking when it came to diversity. He was one of the first designers to feature black models on his catwalk like Donyale Luna and Sandi Collins. And although some ignorant journalists were upset, he paved the way for a more inclusive fashion world.

Pierre Cardin's futuristic glasses

Pierre Cardin

Together with Courreges, Pierre Cardin helped define the space-age look. He made clothes that looked like something out of the Jetsons. He had a love of vinyl, goggles and optical shapes which often appeared both futuristic and wearable. He would continue throughout the sixties making cut out shift dresses, egg carton dresses and helmets.

Thea Porter

Thea Porter started off making cushion coverings with her kaftans. And it dawned on her, that the Kaftans might sell as well. When she began selling them, they became extremely popular with celebrities like Mick Jagger and Sharon Tate. Anyone who was bohemian enough to own one. She expanded her line to make floaty dresses and blouses too. You can spot an original by their floaty sleeves and gorgeous earthy colours with a gypsy style.

Gypsy Dress By Thea Porter in 1969, Willie Christie

Marissa Beneson in Valentino

Valentino

After Valentino Garavani made his fashion debut in 1961, he quickly became the go-to formal dress designer for the glitterati. Jackie Kennedy became friends and wore his designs at all her most important events, including her late sixties wedding where she became Jackie O. Valentino made the colour red his trademark and the fashion house has mastered the colour ever since.

Mondrian Dresses Designed by Yves Saint Laurent

Yves Saint Laurent

When Yves Saint Laurent set up his fashion house in 1961, he didn't know that he would revolutionise fashion instantly. He made ready-to-wear fashion a thing for couture designers. So now the highest-paid and most luxurious designers could make clothes for anyone with enough money to buy them.

He also introduced Le Smoking suit - a tuxedo for women. Something that wouldn't previously be considered feme enough for a woman to wear. Yves loved to mix art with fashion, bringing Pop Art and Picasso to his designs. You may recognise the famous Mondrian shift dress? That was fart (Fashion and art).

7. Fashion On Film

I'm not a fan of reality TV. The people are real, the locations are usually boring and the crying is ugly. If I wanted to see that, I'd just go sit in a Wetherspoons and wait for Garry to have a domestic with his 'missus'. I want to see the unreal. I want aspirational personalities and women who speak like poets. I want to see the gorgeous clothes worn in glamourous locations. And I want tissue-dab-crying. I can find all that in a sixties movie.

I have found this kind of world in several movies that were made in the 1960s. Especially the ones where famous designers like Coco Chanel, Yves Saint Laurent and Mary Quant got involved. If you need a little escape from reality, here's fourteen movies which will take you away to a world where people dress like goddesses. Each film is handpicked for its unforgettable style and influence on sixties fashion.

Film Still Of La Dolce Vita

La Dolce Vita, 1960

This Italian film follows the incredibly intoxicating and indulgent life of a tabloid journalist in Rome. The journalist spends his days mixing with well-dressed aristocrats and stars. The film glamorised the world of the jet setters who flew to parties all over Europe, getting photographed by the paparazzi and looking fabulous while they did it. Expect elegant gowns and cocktail dresses.

Film Still Of A Bout De Souffle

A Bout De Souffle, 1960

American girl Jane Seberg embraces French girl style with her Breton tops and pixie cut. Her look in the film became a template for mod fashion in the years to come. Besides iconic looks, *A Bout De Souffle* made Jean Luc Goddard a well-known director and champion of the French New Wave.

Film Still Of The Millionairess

The Millionairess, 1960

Sophia Loren stars as the millionairess- a businesswoman that is savvy with her money and her fashion. So naturally, every scene serves us impeccable looks from leather belted dresses to fur coats and an abundance of hats. Although, unfortunatly, the look that became famous from the movie is one of her in her undergarments. But she does look hot.

Film Still Of Last Year In Marienbad

Last Year In Marienbad, 1961

If Chanel made movies… well it would be *Last Year In Marienbad*. Chanel collaborated on the French film and personally designed the costumes. Although the film is entirely in black and white, her creations sparkle and shine out from the screen. The leading lady is a vision of money and glamour in her Chanel dresses.

Film Still Of Le Mepris

Le Mépris, 1963

Le Mépris was one of the first French New Wave films that paved the way for art and beauty over the story. Brigitte Bardot takes the starring role of the bored, pouty wife that oozes sexuality in every scene. She wears yellow robes, blue cardigans and striped tops against the beautiful backdrop of Capri. She set the pace for the French mod style.

Film Still Of Darling

Darling 1965

Set in swinging London, we follow a model played by Julie Christie who has a love of A-line skirts and big hair. Throughout the film we see her character's fashion style evolve from small-town girl to queen of the mods. Darling perfectly captures the English women's style of the time.

Film Still Of Blow Up

Blow Up 1966

Blow Up was a British-Italian movie which centres on the life of a fashion photographer, rumoured to be based on Vogue photographer David Bailey. The director enlisted the help of models Verushka and Jane Birkin to showcase the latest fashion in Swinging London.

Film Still Of Qui êtes-vous, Polly Maggoo?

Qui êtes-vous, Polly Maggoo? 1966

This French arthouse movie satirises the fashion world including a take on the notorious Vogue editor Diana Vreeland. Real models, like Donyale Luna and Peggy Moffit, appear in fashion's latest offerings of the French mod fashion world. And even though the film is in black and white, you can still see how great the costume design is.

Film Still Of Belle Du Jour

Belle Du Jour, 1967

Sex, fashion and Paris. This film had everything and it's all dressed up in Yves Saint Laurent. His muse Catherine Deneuve showed us a more conservative French mod at home but by day became a glamorous prostitute. Every look Yves created for the film, screams luxury and elegance.

Film Still Of Two For The Road

Two For The Road, 1967

Naturally, any movie that Audrey stars in, is bound to be fashion gold. In this road trip movie, Audrey plays one half of a couple that takes the same road trip several times throughout their relationship. It's the most fashionable road trip film I've ever seen. We get to watch Audrey waltz around in Paco Rabanne at a glossy party and hang by the pool in Mary Quant. Every piece suits her down to the bone.

Film Still Of Joanna

Joanna, 1968

The story follows a young country girl who travels to London to study fashion. She gets swept up in the Swinging London scene with the fashion, nightclubs and the jet set. *Joanna* serves up a crazy amount of fashion looks on film including a top hat and frilly shirt ensemble. And it shows that London style has evolved from the early sixties into something more avante garde.

8. TV Shows Set In The Sixties

Recently, I found myself lying on my bed surrounded by ready salted crisps. I had been there for hours. I couldn't remember the last time I had got up for anything apart from going to the toilet. Was I sick? No. I had just binged watched the new season of *The Queen's Gambit*, followed by *The Marvelous Mrs Maisel*.

It's not my fault though! They were made to be addictive. I blame Netflix and Amazon for turning me into the slug that I have become. I'm a sucker for watching new sixties TV Shows as well as old movies. When I watch them, I feel like I'm looking through a window into a different time. TV production companies almost always do their fashion history and design the costumes based on originals. So when you're watching these TV series, you're watching one costume designer's version of sixties style.

Film Still Of Mad Men

Mad Men (2007-2015)

If you haven't seen or heard of this TV show then what potato sack have you been living in? Mad Men follows the challenges that faced the advertising industry, from finding out that children shouldn't smoke to the uprising of hippies. Costume designer Janie Bryant won an emmy for her designs on the show. She perfectly captured the career girl style along with the early sixties subruban housewife.

Film Still Of Good Girls Revolt

Good Girls Revolt (2015-2016)

GGR follows the true story of the girls who worked at News Of The Week. The male colleagues thought that women's brains were too small to write and the good girls revolt against them. The show is set at the end of the sixties and the costume designer used mostly dead stock (vintage that hasn't been worn before). So, the clothes are actually real sixties and seventies clothes!

Film Still Of The Marvelous Mrs Maisel

The Marvelous Mrs Maisel (2017-Present)

Ok, they're all not set in New York, I promise. In Mrs Maisel, we get to see what a rising comedian in the sixties looks like. She's joined by her grumpy but lovable manager. Although it seems that Mrs Maisel's opinions are extremely modern for her time, you only have to look at Joan Rivers' sixties comedy acts to see that it's not too far off. Costume designer Donna Zakowska has won two emmys for her suburban housewife designs.

Film Still Of The Queen's Gambit

The Queen's Gambit (2020)

This story follows an orphan who develops a passion for chess. After years of studying and playing the game, she becomes a pro. Though it's traditionally a boys game, she manages to beat them, ignoring the naysayers who say she's too glamorous to be a chess player. And throughout the series, her style develops into an absolute trendsetter from awkward teenager to absolute rock star. Costume designer Gabriele Binder was influenced by Edie Sedgwick and Jean Seberg for her character's style.

Film Still Of 45 Revoluciones

45 Revoluciones (2019)

This Netflix beauty is in Spanish, and if you can't read subtitles, you're weak and natural selection is coming for you. This story follows the establishment of a record label and its very trendy staff. The costume designer goes for a mod look for the leading lady, which perfectly suits her hip surroundings.

9. Vintage

Now you know some sixties style queens, the popular styles, the designers, the boutiques and what sixties clothes look like. Could you spot a genuine sixties dress in your local charity shop?

There are a lot of things about a dress that can give its age away and it doesn't have to be signs of wear. You can have a deeper look at the insides of a dress, trousers or jacket to get a better understanding of when it was made.

One time I found a dress in a vintage shop in Spain. It looked smart with polka dot sleeves and a drop waist. It was marked "60s", which influenced my purchase of course. I bought it straight away and took it home to England.

I showed it to one of my fellow vintage fanatics and she pointed out that it had shoulder pads which were used in the eighties and fourties dresses. Shoulder pads weren't popular in the sixties. Then she pointed out the care label in the bottom half of the dress which said MATALAN in really tiny letters. I had just bought a Matalan dress for £40. I felt like such a mug.

But it was for this reason that I decided to get smart. It prompted me to learn all things I could to spot a genuine sixties dress so I'd never fall for that again.

Hemline

Most dresses in the mid to late sixties were above the knee. A-line shapes were hugely popular in skirts and dresses. Maxi dresses, however, didn't appear until the end of the sixties and were more than likely to be covered in a psychedelic pattern.

Cut

On Sixties dresses, they almost always didn't have a lining. Lining was only used on ladies jackets throughout the era. This was because they still wore slip dresses and underskirts. They also didn't overlock the hem which is a key thing to look out for.

Style

It's always handy to bear in mind your fashion history. When you know what styles weren't popular in the sixties, you'll quickly know if it's a true sixties piece. For example, shoulder pads didn't appear in dresses, womens tracksuits weren't invented and wrap dresses weren't popular until the '70s. Pockets on dresses weren't a thing either. Designers put collars and patch pockets on sixties dresses but they usually weren't for practical use - just decoration.

Fabrics

Towards the end of the sixties, they used a lot of psychedelic prints on man-made fabrics. You'll find a lot of rayon, polyester and nylon. The sixties got a little experimental with fabrics. They used a lot of random things like plastic, PVC, metal and even paper. They began to introduce a lot of fabrics like crimplene, too.

But you could still find a lot of natural fabrics like cotton, cashmere and silks on less economic clothes.

Labels

Every girl loves labels. And if they say they don't? They're lying. Labels are the biggest giveaway of when a piece of clothing was made. It tells you who made it, and by the style of the logo, you can get lost in a google search looking for when it was made. Luckily a lot of designers update and modernise their labels. So you can tell what period it's from. If you need to check a label, head to vintagefashionguild.org who has the biggest collection of vintage labels as a free resource.

Sizing

A lot of people are put off by vintage because of the sizing. They think that vintage is mostly teeny weeny clothes that couldn't possibly fit a modern sized woman. Well, if you're looking for 1920s clothing, you may be right. A larger size is rare.

But sixties clothing? There's more than enough to go around for most sizes. I do come across the occasional teeny weeny size that I'd have to stop eating for five years to fit into but mostly, I find things in all sorts of sizes. Hallelujah.

In the '50s, they used to wear corsets so most dresses from that era have an unnaturally tiny waist. But when it hit the sixties, women were done with that and looked for more comfortable clothes. Fashion was beginning to embrace every size and uniqueness.

But if you find a sixties dress with a size attached to the label, ignore it. Sizing in the sixties is completely different from what it is now. This is where your measurements will come in handy. If you're buying online, ask for the measurements before you buy. Too often, I've bought something that was labelled a 'UK 10' and it arrives with a hamster-sized waist.

If you're in a shop, bring a tape measure, put the clothes against your body or even better, try it on. If you don't, you might buy something that looks more like a top than a dress. Which is also why it's much better to shop in person. Not only can you see the size, but you can feel the fabric and see the stains. You can tell if it's ready to wear or a piece of crap.

Check For Marks

Naturally, the condition will alter the price a lot. I'm not paying £1000 for a vomit-stained kimono, even if Janis Joplin did own it.

Stains are like genital warts, hard to hide and impossible to get rid of. Also look for rips, scorches, mended areas and missing embellishments like buttons. They're all reasons to lower the price. Good, professional online sellers will often point out the damage but always check.

Some nice people in this world try to make our lives easier. Some sellers list their garments under these standard labels: mint (perfection), near mint (almost perfect) excellent (worn but still loved), very good (has its flaws) and good (will make you look bad). If only men came with these labels too.

Accessories

During the movie *Breakfast At Tiffany's*, Audrey Hepburn wears the same black dress several times throughout the movie but yet you don't notice. How come? Accessories of course! Accessories may be small, but they have the power to completely change an outfit. You can even find a modern dress and make it look sixties-style with gogo boots, chunky daisy earrings and a box bag.

White gogo boots

Shoes

One of the most recognised sixties shoe was the beloved gogo boot. A knee high, vinyl textured boot that came in many colours, most popularly, white.

Andre Courrèges was said to have made the original in 1964. His were white, low heeled and came to the mid calf. Andre chose leather to create this very simple but bold style of boot that made fashion headlines.

Shortly after he released his boot onto the world, white boots were being sold everywhere and nicknamed the "go-go". They were made in many different styles and shapes. Longer ones, higher heeled ones and ones in many different colours. Rather than use expensive leather, PVC and vinyl was used. Nancy Sinatra fell in love with them too and made shoe history when she wore them for her song "These Boots Are Made For Walking".

Other popular shoes from the decade included Chelsea boots, Mary Jane strap shoes and practically anything that was flat or low heeled like pumps, brogues, and loafers.

Examples of popular styles of bags in the 1960s

Bags

Although fashion was very futuristic, innovative and abstract during the sixties, the era is not well known for its bags. This is probably because most popular styles were classic shapes from the fifties.

Little box-shaped bags were the most desired for at the time and often seen in the arms of anyone from Brigitte Bardot to Audrey Hepburn. They were a classic square shape made from leather and most commonly fastened with a clasp. The bag had to be big enough to fit in a girl's make up, purse and her latest read.

With the rise of jetsetting, a lot of brands began to make bigger bags to use as baggage holders. Louis Vuitton was the classic option, even then.

Edie Sedwick with her trademark big earrings.

Jewellery

Just like clothes, a lot of jewellery was designed to make a statement. Big chandelier earrings like Edie Sedgwick's were popular throughout most of the sixties and mods would opt for something a bit chunkier than delicate. There were no half measures when it came to jewellery. They were often big, abstract and bold. Hippies, however, loved long jangly necklaces and a mixture of rings. They often looked like they were wearing the contents of an antique jewelry shop.

Brigitte Bardot wearing the popular white framed sunglasses in
the film *L'Ours Et La Poupee*

Sunglasses

Huge, big eyed sunglasses were a big trend in the sixties. From the beginning of the sixties when Audrey Hepburn stepped out of the taxi in her Oliver Goldsmith frames to the end of the sixties with Jackie (newly dubbed) Onnassis.

Popular choices had thick frames in black and white colours but they also came in many other colours. Of course, there was some experimenting with shape too. They tried out asymmetrical sunglasses, heart-shape and thin slitted glasses.

Sometimes, womens fashion borrowed from the boys. Many of the flower children copied John Lennon and wore his trademark circular style glasses.

Jackie Kennedy in a pillbox hat

Hats

The pillbox was invented in the 1930s. It was a round shape with no brim and often made out of wool or felt. Although miliners made them in the thirties, it wasn't until Jackie Kennedy made pillbox hats her thing in the sixties, that they became hugely popular.

Pillbox hats became the hat of the decade. Other hats that were around, but not often associated with the decade. French berets, straw boaters, floppy hats and even plastic rain hats were worn. Anna Karina was a keen lover of hats, often opting for a baker boy, a boater or something wide brimmed in the summer.

Hats were more widely worn in the sixties and some wouldn't leave the house without one.

Sixties advert for tights

Tights

And finally, everyone went crazy for tights in this decade. Patterned, white, multicoloured, floral. You name it. Even the fizzy tights appeared, which later made a comeback in the late '80s and '90s.

At the beginning of the sixties, it was customary to wear tanned coloured tights, but when it turn 1970, girls thought why bother and bare-legged it. It was the bit in between that was the most exciting. A coloured tight can make any outfit look like you're from the 1960s.

Wearing vs Collecting Vintage

I love wearing all my vintage clothes. Which is why I don't have any vintage ball gowns or wedding dresses. I want to buy something and be wearing it the next day. But a lot of people love to build a collection. A collection that is full of pieces that they wouldn't dare wear for a fear of marking them. They hope that their collection would be worthy of a museum one day.

Nothing is wrong with this. It seems quite sensible from a financial point of view. But personally? I like to think about why the clothes were made. Mary Quant didn't design her clothes to hang up in a museum. There are plenty of designers who make clothes for that reason. They're called haute couture. Mary Quant made clothes to be worn all over London. To make the women feel free to bounce around, dance and run all over London. She wanted them to be comfortable. But whatever you decide, love those sixties pieces with all your heart.

10. Care

Unfortunately, our housewife days aren't completely behind us - most of us still have to cook, clean and do the laundry. Maybe one day we'll be rich old ladies with countless vintage Chanel suits and a personal cleaner that will make our clothes smell like sweet cherries, but until then, we have to do it ourselves.

Once you bring home your new sixties dress, you can't treat it like it's fast fashion. This is vintage, darling! You have to treat them like your babies and you have to love them. This will help them look flawless and live another few decades.

Fabrics

First, you need to know the material of the clothes that you're cleaning. If you're unsure of the fabric or are worried about hand washing a garment, always go to the dry cleaner. It's better to pay a bit extra for clean long-lasting clothes than ruin your favourite dress.

Once you know the fabric, here's how to clean it:

Acetate - Dry clean and hang dry.

Acrylic -Machine wash and hang dry.

Corduroy - Turn inside out and machine wash. Tumble dry and can iron when inside out.

Cotton - Whites need to be machine washed on very hot. Colours need the temperature to be warm. Tumble dry and iron.

Crimplene - Hand wash or use the machine's delicate setting with a mild detergent. Air dry.

Denim - Turn inside out and machine wash. Hang dry.

Leather - Send to a specialist dry cleaner and spray with protective leather spray.

Nylon - Wash by hand or machine wash at a cool temperature. Iron cool.

Rayon - Dry Clean.

Silk - Dry clean or hand wash with wool washing liquid but don't rub. Hang dry and steam. If you need to iron, put on a cooler setting and turn inside out.

Spandex - Machine wash at a cool temperature. Hang dry or tumble dry. If you need to iron, put it in a cooler setting.

Suede - Dry clean and spray with suede protector.

Wool and Cashmere - Dry clean or hand wash with wool washing liquid or baby shampoo. Put wool through the machine, only if there is a setting for wool. Hang dry in a steamy bathroom to get rid of wrinkles.

Stains

I'm a messy pup. Whenever I eat, I get most of the food on the floor or down my dress. If I'm drinking wine, somehow I manage to miss my mouth and get it down my front. Overtime, I've accepted that I eat like a baby. Therefore, I've done my absolute best to work out how to get stains out of my clothes. Here are some of my tips:

1. Try and blot it out as soon as it's happened. As soon as you get that spaghetti bolognese stain on your dress, don't carry on eating. Head on to the bathroom and try to blot it out with a white paper towel.

2. If you get stains on your clothes regularly like me, carry around a pocket-sized stain remover.

3. If that doesn't work and it's a machine-washable fabric, buy a pre-wash stain remover, squirt it on and machine wash as usual. If it's a huge stain, run it through the prewash cycle.

4. Spilling alcohol down your dress may look like it didn't stain but it goes a muddy colour if you leave it. Mix warm water and white vinegar and sponge on to the spot. Then launder as normal.

5. Or you can try soaking the garment in the sink with stain remover and gently press the suds through, don't rub.

6. If the stain is greasy, chuck on some talcum powder, leave for a few minutes, then brush off. Then launder on the hottest temperature that the fabric can handle.

But if you're going to eat in your vintage and haven't perfected the art of not dropping food, like me, I do highly recommend wearing a napkin... or a bib.

Storage

When you have a full wardrobe, it can be tempting to bung all your clothes in a pile together or fling them onto any old hanger, but don't. You could be commiting the ultimate sin and damaging your poor vintage clothes.

Depending on the piece, there are many different ways of storing your vintage. Here are the best of my tips:

Hangers - Where you can, use fabric or padded hangers. Plastic, wood and wire can slowly cause damage to most fabrics.

Wool - Don't hang wool otherwise it will stretch. Fold and store in a cool dry place.

Lavender - Wherever you store your clothes, always keep a bag of dried lavender with them. It helps keep away insects like moths (and even spiders!).

Light - Keep all clothes away from the light, the light can deteriorate fabrics over time.

Plastic - Stay away from plastic at all times. Especially don't use it to contain the clothes like bags or boxes- the fabric won't be able to breathe!

Heavy -If your piece is heavy, beaded or fragile, don't hang but fold and put on a shelf or in an acid-free box.

Temperature - Don't store the clothes somewhere that has extreme temperatures. For instance, attics and basements. Store it somewhere where it will be at a comfortable temperature.

Cleaning - Don't wait too long to clean your vintage after wearing. Invisible stains like sweat can gradually damage your clothes if not washed right away.

Customising

Recently, Princess Beatrice arrived on her wedding day in a vintage dress that was originally worn by the queen. The dress had been modernised and it looked beautiful. Big sleeves had been added and the out-dated bubble cut had been removed. It looked 100% better than before.

If you can't tell, I'm all for customising - if it's done right. Princess Beatrice's dress would have been altered by one of the best ateliers in town. Not by someone who's just bought their first sewing machine and fancied giving it a go.

The main reason people think that reworking a dress is a tragedy is because it doesn't come in its true vintage form (and because they believe it will loose its value). This is true if the dress is of historic importance like Audrey Hepburn's Black Givenchy dress. But a St Michael two-piece with a dodgy peplum cut? No one is going to cry if you give it a little snip and modernise it to your tastes. That's what Granny Takes A Trip became famous for.

And if you do come across an iconic piece, sometimes it needs a little bit of work. Maybe the pocket seams are falling apart or a button is missing. Would you just leave it in that sad state? Any good vintage shop will have these minor details sorted for you, but if you're out hunting in charity shops and car boots, you might have to get this done yourself.

I sew myself, but only when the seams have come apart, a button needs adding or the hem needs taking up- mostly for corrections. For anything else, I go to a professional. Look for a tailor experienced in working with vintage. If there isn't one local, then look for a tailor that specialises in bridal wear. Bridal tailors have the expertise to take extra care with delicate fabrics so you'll know your clothes are in safe hands.

Kate Moss always used to take her 1920s vintage flapper dresses to her local tailor and have them hiked up. The result was gorgeous red carpet-worthy dresses. If it's good enough for Kate Moss, it's good enough for you.

11. Get In Loser, We're Going Shopping

By now you should have a good idea what sixties clothes look like, feel like and (probably) smell like. Now it's time for us to take a walk and find some clothes. Start tracking those steps doll because vintage shopping is part of your cardio routine now and by golly, it burns some calories.

Vintage Shops

I'm sure you don't need me to tell you, but there's guaranteed vintage in these kinds of shops. They're the best place to look at vintage because the shop owner is usually an expert on the clothes they've curated AND they know what they're talking about (I hope anyway). They sometimes date all of the clothes for you so you don't have to work out whether it's a sixties or seventies dress. If they're friendly they can even give you tips on looking after the clothes. I would highly recommend beginning your sixties journey in a vintage shop. Get familiar with sixties clothes. Find your favourite styles or designers. Memorise the labels. Touch the fabrics. See the stitches.

Online Shops

Most bricks and mortar shops have online shops too, if they know what's good for them. Online, you can find vintage shops from all over the world and it feels like a neverending variety. But with a bigger selection comes a lot of naff stuff too. Some shops are even trying to pass off Primark for Paco Rabanne (I've actually seen one Primark dress sell for £60).

The best rule of play when you're starting is to go for a fully established online shop who is credible and easily contactable. *cough* like my sixties boutique on Mandy-Morello.com *cough*. And, have you still got your measurements from before? Check them against the shop's listing to avoid having something delivered that doesn't fit.

Charity Shops

I recently headed out to a charity shop in a quiet village in the south of England and found the most gorgeous 1960s linen shift dress, just hanging there amongst the riff-raff for £6.99. I couldn't believe my eyes. I quickly took it to the counter and almost ran out the shop, just in case the owner changed her mind. This is why charity shops are the most rewarding. It feels like you've found treasure.

But, charity shop owners are getting savvier. Sometimes, they'll have a vintage rack in the shop. But if you know your stuff down to the core, you can spot the treasures that they've mistaken for modern day crap.

I have often found that in the postcodes with more expensive housing have better quality clothes in the local charity shops. But that doesn't mean you can't find a gem in other areas too. I believe it's better to search for vintage in smaller towns and villages. London is rife with vintage shoppers so you'll be lucky to find anything there unless you're out at silly hours of the morning.

Charity shopping may take a long while to find anything decent. But if you love looking through racks and racks of clothes in search of something special, it will be worth it. And do I have to remind you that it's great for cardio. Are you still tracking those steps?

Car Boot Sales

Sometimes, you'll find a lovely woman, who has a ton of clothes that don't fit her anymore but she's hung on to them because she loved them. They reminded her of her youth. These were the clothes she met her husband in or when she went to her first dance and the dress she got married in. And finally, today, she's decided to let them go and brought her wardrobe to a car boot sale.

You assure her, you'll look after her babies. And if she likes you, she might give you her whole collection of sixties mini skirts for

£20. She was only going to take it down the tip later if they didn't sell anyway.

Even if you don't come across the holy grail of car boot sellers like this one, you'll meet lots of lovely people, have a great day out and may spot something else you love. Like a pastel teapot or a couple of tennis rackets. Most frequent shoppers at a car boot tend to go for the electrics. Leave the boys to their toys, and grab the things with real value; vintage.

Auction Houses

So in America, a lot of fashionistas go to Estate sales. From my experience, they don't do a lot of that here in England. When an older lady leaves behind all of her personal belongings, the family either pays a clearance man who takes them to auction (sometimes online auctions), throws a car boot sale or donates them to charity.

Auction houses mostly auction off jewellery, antiques and bric a brac. I would do your research before attending an auction as you might end up sitting through hours of mundane auctions and find no clothes. Look out for special clothes auctions and events. Once Geri Halliwell took all her Spice Girls dresses (including that Union Jack dress) and auctioned them all off. That Union Jack dress sold for £36,200.

Relatives

And finally, if you have some fashionable relatives, always ask to have a look in their wardrobes. We women can be quite the hoarders, so guaranteed there is something in one of your friends or family's closets that they've harboured on to but never let go. More often than not, they'd be delighted to see it find new life in your wardrobe.

Unlucky for me, my mother was quite cutthroat with her wardrobe. She used to chuck things out all the time and replace it with new things. When I raided her wardrobe, I found nothing but new dresses, her favourite jeans and absolutely nothing over two years old.

Which is why you should branch out to other relatives too, don't just stop at your mum. Or chat with friends. Once I started my vintage boutique, I was surprised at how many of my friends offered to give me their vintage clothes that either didn't fit them anymore or weren't loved like they used to be.

Put yourself out there. Have a look for local swap parties too. They're where girls meet up and swap their old clothes for someone else's. Don't limit yourself. Look everywhere.

12. Sixties Revivals

Recently, I picked up a gorgeous cream shift dress in my local vintage shop. It had the most detailed lace pattern on it with absolutely no stains. It had no label but it had lining. As we were learned earlier, they didn't tend to use lining in sixties dresses. But it looks exactly like a sixties outfit? So how come?

Well, you've probably guessed it already. It's a revival. There are a lot of sixties-inspired clothes out there today. Using the information in this book, you'll begin to spot the differences.

But, being a newer version of a sixties shift dress doesn't make it less desirable. A gorgeous sixties-style dress is a gorgeous sixties-style dress.

Stevie Nicks continuing the 'hippie look' in 1975

The Seventies

When it hit the end of the decade, people didn't suddenly fling off their shift dresses and shimmy straight into a sequin jumpsuit. A lot of the early seventies still had the look and style of the late sixties. Biba was still running, Twiggy was still waltzing around with her Bambi legs and we hadn't seen the last of Paco Rabanne's disc dresses.

The hippie look was still on trend until midway through the seventies. And mods continued for the other half of the decade, especially when The Who released their movie Quadrophenia in 1979.

Jane Fonda in popular 1980s activewear

The Eighties

The eighties took a step away from the world of the sixties and stepped back to the 1940s with shoulder pads and peplum silhouettes. Women could be seen dressing in power suits and big hair. It was time to get physical! In came activewear in the form of tracksuits, leggings and leg warmers. Barbarella actress Jane Fonda became a huge advocate.

Shirley Manson in her shift dress in the music video 'I'm Only Happy when It Rains'

The Nineties

The sixties came back but in a big way. Think Shirley Manson, Spice Girls or Oasis. They paired their shift dresses and mini skirts with fishnets and platform shoes. They wore their tea dresses with big black boots and used the slip dress as outerwear. For me, this is my favourite revival of the sixties style. The ninetiess were all about experimenting, customising and being different.

Moschino 2013 Spring Ready To Wear

The 2000s - Today

When the millennium arrived, fashion was anyone's game. It was all about street style and everyone was mish-mashing the influences from every era. Fast fashion was now flourishing.

You can now find a lot of sixties-inspired designs on the high street but they'll be poorly made compared to 20th Century clothing. The fast fashion age tends to use cheaper materials and poorly structured designs. They're created to be thrown away, which is why you'll find that they don't last decades.

But it's not all doom and gloom in the modern world. There are still designers that love to produce quality, sustainable sixties-style clothes. Even if Moschino is out of your budget, there are some smaller independent designers out there that will cater to you. Some of my favourites are Miracle Eye, Hippie Shake and Mod Cloth.

13. Go Wild

For a long time I never 'dressed vintage' because I was worried what people would say. I thought that they'd either laugh or whisper about how ridiculous I looked. So I stuck to plain boring clothes for far too long, and stuck to not wearing anything that was out of the ordinary.

After a while, plain tops and jeans weren't cutting it for me. It was like I was pretending to be someone else. There I was, sitting in my bedroom, scrapbooking mod fashion and swooning over vintage copies of Vogue while I was dressed in a Von Dutch hat and plain jeans. So I decided to begin my journey into sixties clothes.

I started by purchasing vintage-inspired clothes from the high street and layering with sixties-style accessories that are still popular today like berets or big statement earrings. But I became tired of modern fast fashion and longed for something a little more authentic. I started looking for original pieces.

At first, I made the big mistake of just buying anything with a vintage stamp on it, just because it was vintage. But after some time, I realised I had a wardrobe full of clothes that either didn't fit me or made me feel uncomfortable. Remember the high waisted jeans I told you about earlier? It was time to do a massive clear out.

That's when I discovered a sixties magazine article about the rules of balance in fashion. The sixties essentially taught me how to dress for my body shape. I began investing in sixties pieces that I knew would look great on me. I noticed that whenever I get dressed in the morning, it had become as easy as licking a lollipop. Any piece I pulled out now fitted me perfectly and made me feel more like myself.

It turned out that no one did laugh at my new look and no one called me ridiculous like I thought they would. In fact, I had more compliments than ever. But, I had realised something even more profound than that. I didn't care what anyone thought of my outfits because the clothes made me feel free.

Keep Your Mind Open

I didn't get to this state of fashion euphoria with just my limited knowledge of clothes. I branched out to different styles and looks, seeing how each one suited me. I found that the hippie look didn't suit my personality and the Audrey Hepburn look was far too reserved. It took a few trials before I fell in love with the French version of mods and the cutesy colours of the dolly girls. I wouldn't have found what I loved without trying everything.

The most important thing to do is experiment with your clothes. Pick up things that look wacky and that you've never worn before. You might risk looking like a clown but sometimes you'll be surprised how great things look on you, rather than on a hanger. So try everything on.

Don't even just stick to the usual fabrics. Experiment with materials like they did in the sixties. Don't shy away from plastic coats and paper dresses, it might be your best look yet.

Twist & Shout

I hated school uniforms with a passion. Or any uniform for that matter. They make me feel like I'm a robot with no thoughts of my own. So, when I was at school, I'd rebel a little bit by adding badges or wearing bright coloured nail polish to make me feel more like me. Sometimes that would earn me detention, but it was worth it.

I did the same with sixties clothes. You don't have to go head to toe in sixties gear and look like a carbon copy of Anna Karina. Try and give every look your own little twist. Edie Sedgwick was the queen of twists. She'd wear the latest looks with her signature big earrings. And she made thick tights with a top her thing. Your thing could be sixties beehives with lilac hair or mini skirts paired with leather jackets. The possibilities are endless. Find your signature twist and try to mix it into whatever you wear.

Just remember, every single piece in your wardrobe is YOURs. Every item's purpose is to make you look and feel good. If it doesn't make you feel good, can you customise the clothes so it works for you? If you can't, bin it (or take it to your local charity).

A lot of the girls in the sixties didn't stick rigidly to trends, they made it their own. They experimented. Don't be afraid to try new things and talk with a tailor. Maybe your crazy idea of turning a prairie dress into a co-ord set can be done. Never stay in the box.

Make Your Own Kind Of Music

One last note. Once you find your style, remember it when you're going shopping. It's easy to get carried away with the latest trends or your local boutique's new sixties stock. Just because it's an original sixties babydoll dress, it doesn't mean you have to buy it.

Always ask yourself; is it your style? Can you make it your style? Does it look good on you? And most importantly, does it make you feel great? If you answer no, put it back on the hanger and walk away.

Sixties clothes and modern day trends come and go, but your own personal style lasts forever.

About Mandy Morello

Mandy Morello is a writer who is obsessed with talking about anything to do with the sixties. She shares regular free content on www.Mandy-Morello.com where she also sells her personal collection of vintage.

When she's not writing and packing more vintage clothes into her suitcase, you can find her living like it's the sixties on social media.

Instagram: @Mandy_Morello.